MW00743942

Our Highest Priority

Our Highest Priority

Embrace Courage, Abandon Fear

By
Marva A. Smith

Strategic Book Publishing and Rights Co.

Strategic Book Publishing and Rights Co.
12620 FM 1960, Suite A4-507
Houston, TX 77065
www.sbpra.com

For information about special discounts for bulk purchases, please contact Strategic Book Publishing and Rights Co. Special Sales, at bookorder@sbpra.net.

ISBN: 978-1-63135-392-5

Dedicated to the memory of
Edmund, Geraldine, Anthony, Hersey, David
and Una Lammy

Table of Contents

Angel 'A' and Angel 'B'

Two frisky angels sitting in a tree

With nothing to do but cause havoc and melee,

Decided to play a game on humanity.

Said Angel 'A' to Angel 'B'

"What mischief, prithee, can we bring to keep us busy?"

Said 'B' to 'A',

"What will be your name?"

"Expectation!"

"What will be your game?"

"Complication!"

"And where will you live?"

"In everyone's life!"

"What will be your aim?"

"To make everyone wise!"

'A' to 'B',
"What will be your name?"
"Characterization!"
"What will be your game?"
"Explanation!"
"And where will you live?"
"In everyone's life!"
"What will be your aim?"
"To make everyone wise."

So, with much glee and delight
They circled as they flew, pondered
And considered with energy anew;
They flittered and twittered,
The sky it turned blue,
Until at last, 'B' asked,

"What's the name of the trick?"

"Relationship!"

"What rules will apply?"

"Apple of the eye!"

"Which wish will come first?"

"Desire to quench a thirst!"

"And how shall we start?"

"With an arrow through the heart!"

Oh, they danced and they pranced

With a passion all renewed, and off they flew

With Cupid 'The Stupid' behind them.

Their prey unsuspecting

Was found humanly selecting

An apple in the Garden of Eden.

Aye! So the story goes, and now everyone knows

The greatest of the three is Love!

It is not easy but it's free,

Grows like a weed on a vine of dichotomy,

Expected of Cupid's arrow on a wild spree,

Complicated by the hazing,

Characterized by the havoc it is raising,

Explained by the mirth of Angel 'A' and Angel 'B'.

In the Heat of the Night

In the heat of the night
An audacious desire took flight,
Braving denizens of the deep
Somersaulted into my sleep.

Vivid visions marvelled my eyes
Vibrant colours transformed the sky,
Dancing revellers dressed in gold
Waving banners as centuries unfold.

Momentous emotions stirred my dreams as
I wriggled and reached to capture something.
Flickering fires lit scene after scene
Painting passionate pictures upon a screen.

Frame after frame with confidence and command
A portrait portrayed how the world began
With love and devotion hour after hour
The Almighty creates to an infinite power.

Ancient symbols many a parable told
Of a dream conceived radical and bold.
With verve and vigour for truth and adventure
An idea was formed in a physical manner.

Laws of nature with miraculous spontaneity
Balanced forces of energy as principles of gravity,
Sacred themes of Faith, Love and Compassion,
Foundation beams for a system based on action.

The Vortex

Heady moments heavily populated my dream
Enthusiastically informing me with thoughts supreme.
Vaulting into the vortex created by my ardent desire
Illumination dawned at the assembling of this cosmic empire.

Exuberant playfulness one imaginary day
Envisioning games magnificent beings love to play,
Filled the atmosphere with elements of intellectual sustenance
Highly integrated galaxies sprung completely into existence.

Fields full of fruits and flowers, fishes swimming upstream,
Variety in this spectacular environment fulfills the eternal dream.
Wisdom, opportunity, timing, possibility, all
Specialties within our capacity to realize our true potentiality.

Fascinated, my mind fastened on this video stream
Revealing a great conundrum to the universal dream.
Building blocks of ideas, concepts, interweaved
Refining philosophies, profound thoughts, high ideals.

Giddily as flowers roaring riotously into bloom
Uproariously erupting into colours and dizzying perfume;
Frisky and frolicsome as lambs playing in Summer weather,
Gaily galloped my thoughts as freed horses in a meadow.

Around and around in a circle wide they flew,
Busily stretching and exercising sinews anew.
Such exuberant spirits burgeoned within my dream
Superior thoughts bubbling and rising, pressing against the seams.

Enlightenment

Extraordinary!
My imagination seemed infused with some newly invented speech,
Having risen to a level that is ordinarily out of reach – with
Supreme organization its sequencing shrewdly eschewed chaos,
And smoothly my messianic desire continued where it left off:

Universes are formed with a strategic design
To maintain and renew the state of mankind;
Whole spheres of music and mathematics supply
The necessary knowledge the world twirls by.

Whirls of numbers, formulas given life,
Measuring matter – a scientific device.
Solid and liquid interacting in space, survival
Material? Or employment for the human race!

Cataloguing and categorizing, an unbounded responsibility,
Sense of humour coupled with bustle promotes camaraderie;
Intense emotions intertwined with a zest to be the best propel
Competitors into realms to reach for the heights of success.

Melodious sounds awaken our inner senses
Sharpen our skills and quicken our natural defences,
Their healing power entertains and elevates
The spirited tones of the heart it regenerates.

My heightened sensations pulsed with urgency for information,
Divining plans and methods for communication.
Models aglow with intuitive abilities to capture
The dawn of enlightenment, revelation and rapture.

The Buzz

Buzzing with ambition to pursue this opportunity,
Impulses leapt, synapses snapped smartly into bustling activity.
Instincts that activate our fantastic ability to concentrate
Instantly stimulate that refining quality to ameliorate.

Efflorescing, my mind soared with astounding abandon,
Deftly guided by my quixotic companion.
Vistas of landscapes blossomed spontaneously into view,
Flourishing and fragrant, flexible with cooperative glue.

Ecstatically, my entire body quivered with exquisite delight
Surrendering to answers and penetrating insights. Surreptitiously,
This transporting process climbed to even higher heights
Orchestrating timeless messages with super-rapturous flight.

The Rapture

Relationship as a concept or as an expression
Is an element of measurement in nature's function;
Its rule of action enables cooperation and
Its reach stretches throughout creation. It is
An underlying principle of communication,
A foundation that links boundless populations;
Infinite in its combinations and associations
It is incalculable and incomprehensible to fathom.

Nature's function is one of accommodation,
A vital force in its quest for equilibrium;
Its versatility coheres to all in existence and its
Dexterity maintains constancy of the environment.
These processes initiate a need for conformity
Through continuous combinations universal in reality;
These associations promote affinities
Relationships measured by their similarities.

The universe is patterned on self-regulation
Aspect of discipline based on repetition.
Timing tools for accuracy and predictability
Are innate controls for command and quality.
These characteristics instill a sense of rhythm
Echoes in relation to dynamics of creation,
Such reverberations promote a state of fitness:
Embodiment essential in robust relationships.

Rhapsody

The world functions on a vision of hope:
Fearless belief that all dreams will succeed;
These desires give rise to a sense of expectancy
Emotional quality inherent in reality;
These feelings energize the senses –
Faculties of perceptive and intelligent influences,
Such unique abilities empower every one individually
To live harmoniously, yet competitively in society.

Every society functions on framework of regulations
Designed by public institutions to organize population,
These rules are enforced by governing bodies
Power exercised by legal authorities.
Such discipline is applied in all forms of activity
Religious, political, commercial, community;
This behaviour is universal in its application
Uniting nations on the foundation of civil relations.

All social relationships share community spirit
Emotional energy nourished by status or merit;
These attributes glorify certain positions, elevated by
Occupation, education or other related affiliations.
Such groupings can incur feelings of superiority, a
Distinction applied to regions favoured by geography. These
Distinguishing elements can create a sense of imbalance
Through trade, knowledge, or economic circumstance.

Communities are composed of diverse families
Each member equipped with skills and ability;
Such talent fires up a need for expression in
Relation to age, generation and cause of dissention.
These instances require a certain vision and
Communication to sow seeds for reparation.
This form of innovation drives momentum and
Support reinforced by majority of population.

Families are the foundation of society,
Each established on rules by graded authority;
This hierarchic method mirrors the trinity –
Practice exhibited throughout reality.
Such organizational plans foster dependency
Nurturing trust, cooperation necessary in families;
These beneficial qualities build healthy relationships
Inspiring moral excellence and cohesive fellowship.

Relationships are incalculable and incomprehensible to fathom
They all have the same characteristics in common;
Each is endowed with same possibilities for success
Motivated by same opportunities, drive and stress.
These powerful forces jostle with degrees of intensity
Competing with each other with boldness and urgency;
Such emotional qualities are unequally balanced
Causing unpredictable and unexpected circumstance.

Partnership

Friendship is an attachment that I cannot fathom,
I wonder if it felt the same for Eve and Adam?
Understanding their feelings, give or take, confusion!
Engaging with each other as lovers or companions.
These are the vagaries of friendship
Peculiarities that exist in every relationship;
Decisions tumultuous in the making,
Breathtaking in the undertaking.

Relationship is progressive behaviour,
It has to be progressive to survive;
Modelled by father and mother, but
First defined by husband and wife.
As these two individuals together
Begin their journey through life, their
Romance predicts their principal agreement, do they
Share partnership, or are they ruled by dictatorship?

Empirical data advance the idea
Casual observation confirms what they say:
That most couples entering into a relationship
Spend little time discussing their partnership, and
Much to their chagrin they make certain assumptions
Based on the idea of their idea of the other person.
Experience is not always the best judge of character
A deep discussion will deliver what you are after.

Sometimes unlikely couples settle for one another
Merging feelings with reasons for being together;
This crafts their union into a plan where
Opportunities for renewal are often at hand.
This relationship is usually one filled with joy
From equal partnering couples employ.
An alliance based on mutual respect
A symbiosis made for a happy prospect.

Expectation

Relationships develop for brilliant reasons
All created in extraordinary ways, some
Friendships survive for many seasons, after
Decades they disintegrate on faulty ideas.
But each relationship explores its own topic
Using every individual with their own logic,
And as circumstances demand
Challenging situations come to hand.

Every friend has their own expectations:
Reasoning based on their own need and motivation,
Perceptions pursued with unyielding precision
And determination to gain complete satisfaction.
Regard the decision to build a budding friendship
Shaping a personality to your vision of relationship,
Time spent with each other, opinions exchanged,
Whose interests will continue to fan this flame?

Curiousity can be a powerful factor
Attracting attention of a persuasive motivator,
Will this phenomenon be a long-lasting mechanism,
Maintaining attentiveness of an exploring dynamism?
Charm and intelligence is also a winning combination
One without the other can be a monotonous drain,
These and any number of positive characterizations
Invigorate one's optimism and alleviate any strain.

Individual Adventure

Friendship is always an individual adventure
Personalities united in a shared idea together.
Sometimes their purpose is truly profound
And longevity in the relationship is prolonged.
But in the case of a tenuous strand when all
Hands are searching for a stronger bond
That's when we each need to recognize
Every friendship has its own reasons to survive.

All relationships fit into their own categories
Organized by their differences or similarities.
Each classification reveals the usual refrain
Fascination with a personality's pain.
Seldom do they chronicle suitable solutions
Or success in conquering their own situation;
Exultation experienced by some human beings
Or inspiring progress advanced by accomplishing.

It is within the nature of every relationship
To present challenge in the form of fellowship,
A fundamental element, an equivalent ingredient
Forms the foundational equation for every friendship.
Every situation requires some type of association
Connection to strengthen growth and communication
Between all species: plants, animals and human beings –
A union that exists between the seen and the unseen.

It is this connection between all living beings
That provides a springboard for related things;
The allure of a positive attraction or
Magnetism of a negative reaction.
In either case we become stuck like glue
Hardly daring to research the truth,
Our instincts may prod another point of view
But we feel chained to the path which we pursue.

Every individual symbolizes their own cause in action,
Preparation for their stage of growth and projection;
This yearning lies within our own personal ambition,
A motivational key triggering all our own decisions.
These deeper desires direct us in all our goals
Tracking our achievement as our progress unfolds;
Experiences are designed to strengthen our resolve
And advance us in our quest to conquer our cause.

Family Dynamics

In relationships with our parents, they
Say babies from the time of their birth
Compete on some level with a parent
That earns them a wrathful curse.
This is such a ludicrous idea
That deserves a laughable outburst,
But really, as some families rule
Consequences are painfully true.

Examine relationship between brother and sister
Or, father and mother for that matter;
They are the closest ties kinship enjoys but
Are they reasons good friendship employs.
Challenge lies within family structure
And twin observation of human nature,
How personalities develop their drive and
Conform to philosophies their logic derides.

Mother and father, their rules may differ
Being generous to brother but denying sister.
Their reasons explained may be superficially sane
But suppression here is the name of that game.
On every side resentment resides –
No matter the gain, everyone's in pain;
Guilt by enjoyment or guilt through restraint,
No one here can escape the blame.

A parent's unequal application of generousity
Heightens a family's sense of superiority;
Parents, hopefully, are wiser beings
But why the brother since he is still growing?
Sister, by default, develops inferiority
Accommodating a preference for conformity,
While parents, rarely, on the other hand,
Show understanding for her lack of enthusiasm.

Schism

Of course this approach promotes a schism
Superiority conferred by favouritism.
This type of division sums up our discord
In every form of society records record.
Simple observation – treatment of the sexes
Reveals paternalism reigns, feminism vexes,
While relationships reported from every corner
Show cracks and crevices – a suppressive disorder.

Pattern of expectation: submit to conformity
Following rules that exist in every society.
The view is not to be seen as "out of place"
But to be in unity with the human race.
Such thinking is accepted as from the Divine,
Executed with blessing of sanctified wine;
Anyone who dares step out of line is
Accused of being in a conspiracy design.

Our Purpose Here

Based on our gender
We develop certain behaviours and
Employ a stigma we apply to each other
To ensure conformity to rules of society.
With every personality rebelling
Some individuals feel lured into escaping
Those rigid demands and influential pressures
Authority groups inject into their letters.

These biases are everywhere – universal,
One group seeks rules to reinforce
Another group, same rules, seeks a reversal,
Of course there is always one that stays neutral!
We've created, under these circumstances, a
Perfect situation for graded ambivalences – the
Question remains, what rules should society maintain
With its citizens for a seamless order to reign?

The only society that seems justified, is
One where equal opportunity for all can reside.
The challenge this philosophy provides should
Promote best efforts from its citizens to survive.
Early education should be grounded in this thinking,
Competitive efforts should be levelled at achieving,
Career happiness should be aimed at perceiving highest
Quality of living every resident should be pursuing.

Our purpose here is to meet every challenge
Disguised in the form of relations and alliance.
Every point of view is observed and strategized
Every approach followed through fully to satisfy.
Consequences of our actions are lessons to teach
Each one of us suitable solutions needed to reach
Compassion and understanding for loving and living
Between all creatures, organisms and human beings.

Creating Magic

Every relationship creates its own magic
Based on personalities' personal habits.
Arm in arm we link on a truth
That is not necessarily fair to any of us.
My need for friendship may target a risk-taker
Someone who can help me become an innovator.
Your need may be for someone of another hue
Perhaps a chameleon to fit any version of you.

Clearly our expectation of each other
Has potential to be a perfect disaster; would
Solid discussion of each other's character
Help to avert a disappointing encounter?
If both of us are faithful to our nature and
From each other expect reasonable behaviour,
Then, to all intent, we can call it a truce and
Wave our flag to show a friendship that's true.

We may then find a mutual arena, where,
As kindred spirits we can agree together
To compete or conduct another arrangement
More suitable to both of our own temperaments.
This approach is composed with skillful artistry,
Desire for excellence in each other's competency.
Like-minds configured on the battlefield
Every one displaying their talent in the deal.

Each one of us then goes our own separate direction
Discovering hints and clues to our own individuation;
Through subtlety or anxiety we ascertain signs
To establish us on the path that moulds our minds.
Our journey then, is a manifestation of those times,
Age, period and phase, its development has designed.
Every one of us, with true distinction, fingerprints the plan
Stamping it with our own uniquely contributing brand.

Jealousy

A relationship based on jealousy cannot survive
It takes energy and integrity to keep hope alive.
Sincerity in our desire and our pride comes from
Knowledge that our talent too will be recognized.
Enjoyment comes when our muscles are strained in
Competition where we experience the greatest gain.
When friend meets foe and they are evenly matched
Success comes with the quickest dispatch.

Jealousy is a deviation from competitive spirit, each
One of us arrives in the world to compete fully equipped.
Our challenge is to find our area of expertise then
We can blast through our path with relative ease.
But when square peg meets round hole and chafes
'There is no traction to get a grip,'
On this trail it finds itself very unfit; will the
Player then reorganize for a different trip?

But jealousy can be a motivating factor –
Energy to be harnessed like a nuclear reactor,
Using that thrust as an explosive burst propels
You up the ladder to achieve what you're after.
In that case you have entered the race,
Your ability to perform should be above your norm,
Competitors competing will not alter their pace
Your entry should be made with confidence and haste.

Competition here resembles high-powered behaviour
You are now in the sphere of rarefied air.
Attention is paid to technique and training
Observation of the rules and creative gaming.
Skirmishes and tackles, aggressive contact,
Players are charging, opponent's at your back,
No time to whine, relax, or be displeased,
Opportunity should be seized with consummate ease.

Creativity

Artistry and bravery, aspects of creativity –
Implements and devices used in every industry.
Planning and timing, strands of flexibility
Stretching the capacity of one's dexterity.
Acuity in game comes from depths of awareness
Skill and patience are legitimate deeds of fairness;
The stakes at this point not for the faint of heart,
A fool and his money are soon torn apart.

This level of play requires mental stamina,
Competitors aware of stress they are under.
Confidence and concentration, tools at your command
Neutralizes pressure and firms the hand.
Critics commenting on your game each play
May characterize it in highly critical ways;
In this league, your ability to accept defeat
Will be measured as an aspect of your conceit.

Craftsmanship and shrewdness, artistic skills;
Cunning and crudeness, mediocre thrills.
Your level of play is revealed in the form of
Preparation and methods you use to disarm.
Marketplace arrayed with products for trade,
Savvy buyers and vendors of every age,
Competition is fierce and grows at hectic pace
But the smartest performer captures the race.

Smart performers are assessed by their plays,
Using perception and instinct as penetrating rays;
They haven't necessarily passed all the tests in
Schools and universities that produce the best,
But they are versatile in application of their skills
Pursuing their prey with concentrated will,
Eagerly studying all the trading details
Targeting their audience for a persuasive sale.

Friendship

Friendship, like a filament, is difficult to fathom,
A tenuous strand in the relations of man.
If taken for granted its longevity is aborted,
If disrespected, then trust is thwarted.
Assumptions and expectations, always on trial,
Avoidance and evasions, patterns of denial.
Yearning for warmth in bosom of someone's esteem,
A clasp to the heart, fulfillment of a dream.

Friendship is a form of social activity
Wining and dining, sipping tea and coffee.
Exchange of conversation, pat on the back,
Smiling, embracing, signs of giving back.
But this illusion is somewhat obfuscated by
Glitter and conflicting symbols, how is that related
In an atmosphere of bon vivant full of joie de vivre
Displaying scenes of animousity rife with hateful rivalry?

This is another face of friendship
Expressed in competitive terms,
We can neither hide nor disguise it
A feeling we can all discern.
Competition keeps the planets spinning in their orbits,
A perceptive view of cooperation in a system we all inhabit.
It's an intense force regulated to our level of discourse; an
Invisible, inexhaustible tension that sustains our imagination.

Too often we see competition in a narrow view
Forgetting it has a larger, more vigourous truth,
As in the competing nature of our cells to grow,
Our ideas to expand and build the world we know.
Our world is permeated by that foraging spirit, a
Positive and optimistic force that lives within it.
It is the nature of our nature everything to contest,
With diligence and effort to be the best.

Competition

Competition, an invigorating force
Designed to elevate our level of discourse.
As flavourful seasonings heighten our taste,
So does excitement spice up the race –
Hand to hand combat, one team against another,
Spectators all cheering, rooting for their player;
It's an ancient strategy to muster citizens' support
To build a cohesive nation and boost national rapport.

Competition among nations, another tenuous strand,
Exhibited primarily in their weapons at hand,
Their ability to trade and their treaties for aid.
A warrior's mind is shown in their military might,
A build-up of arms for a contest to fight.
Diplomatic relations, another competitive tact;
Which nation will negotiate which rules to relax?
What price will relations among nations exact?

A fact that is universal –
A government's resistance to interference. Any
Competing idea is an opportunity for political play
Leaders will claim its opposition's intent to defame
And launch a merciless attack
On its citizens who dare to fight back.
This is another face to a political race, the
Nature of a game not for the timid or the tame.

Politics is played in every corner of the universe. In every
Industry, with every creature, competition quenches a thirst.
Every mind desires to wield power of some kind! As a
Tool for survival it drives the effort for revival; it's a
Measure of conviviality for connoisseurs and the savvy.
Some rules are entrenched over centuries and time spent
As in hunting traditions and sporting cultures; but as
An event, competition is an ebullient element in nature.

Discipline and Desire

Discipline in competition, an exacting demand,
Control of the game is power in the hand.
A sportsman in his play is exciting in the game
When discipline and zeal are revealed as the ideal.
Passion produces the power to overcome defeat,
A driving, determined ambition to succeed.
As scientists formulate formulas to eradicate disease
Competitors use desire to energize their efficiency.

Complexity in the game demands dexterity in the play;
An artist at hand renders a drawing for display capturing
Confidence and concentration, signs of basic training,
Preparation for the game, aspects of discipline.
Quick thinking is fundamental in basic technique,
Practice programs the muscles to perform this feat.
Consistency in rehearsal polishes the skills
For smooth execution and delightful thrills.

Discipline in combat, life-saving acts,
Quickens the mind, sharpens the contact.
Keen awareness of enemy in environment at hand
Trains attention for sounds, whispered commands;
Stealthy footfalls, rustles in the brush,
Hair-trigger movements, hearts beating in a rush;
Timing and breathing, discipline and training,
Combined with action, overpowering combinations.

Preparation for situations demands mental discipline;
Quick thinking, anticipation, are spontaneous reactions.
Circumstances designed to confuse and complicate
Plans and important matters trigger a sense of panic;
Deep breathing to calm and return a feeling of balance
Restores equilibrium, strengthens one's confidence.
This mental acuity reinforces our sense of sanity
Allowing us to rejoice at the dexterity of our ability.

Celebration

Enjoyment is a fundamental element in all relationships
All creatures enjoy some happiness in their friendships.
Animals relate to grooming for respect and love's sake,
Showing affection and creating peaceful relations.
Birds sing, harmonizing everything,
Thrilling notes that float from spring to eternal spring.
Trees with their branches provide shade and covering
Beautifying the world – fruitfully feeding and flowering.

All seasons display signs of discipline,
Each season in its own due time, returning.
Sometimes in their ritual they delight and surprise
Timing their appearance by bursting in reverse;
Especially winter appearing at height of summer
And then we think matters cannot get worse,
Or when our internal balance is thrown out of kilter
With a heat wave descending in the depths of winter.

This is nature at its romping best,

Challenging us to push ourselves to meet its test,

To slough off our own sense of complacency

Our own ritualistic dance that breeds despondency;

Nature inviting us to celebrate and to party

Any season, every season, and all year round,

You see, it neither matters the time nor the clime,

Enjoyment and celebration are gifts from the Divine.

Rhythm of Vibration

Discipline as a tool is designed to enforce rules,
It is also a tool to break those rules.
Nature, as nature dictates, leads by natural example
Using random selections as reinforcing samples.
These magical images and ideas meant to introduce
A humourous side of its gifts for our occupational use.
What better way to capture our vibrant imagination by
Varying the many wonders of these fantastic creations!

Discipline in music echoing through the ear,
Sensations vibrating at a rhythmic pace,
Emotions respond by picking up a trace of
Pheromones perfuming and scenting the air.
Romance blossoming in attractive atmosphere,
Creatures partnering, having love affairs;
Creation's solution to appreciating and sharing
Gifts and graciousness of this habitable sphere.

All bodies respond in communicative ways,
Whispering and waving, signals we all share.
Fishes swimming in depths of the ocean
Keenly attuned to the rhythm of vibration.
Trees identify objects by vibratory signature
Objects respond same within Mother Nature.
Vibration is key, secret of the Divine
Every possible thing reacts in vibratory time.

Discipline is the glue that keeps us from unravelling
Radio waves provide clues, pulsating while transmitting.
Vibration is the effect, measured by its speed,
Transforming energy into objects, meeting populations' need.
Animals respond to vibration of the earth
Signalling storms or water to quench their thirst.
Heartbeats like drumbeats synchronized by rhythmic bursts,
Communicating messages of goodwill, or sometimes worse.

Repetition

Repetition is essential to discipline's design,

A tension that automatically maintains earth's time.

With regulatory precision mathematically devised,

It's a harmonious system, a uniting device.

Repetition features prominently within Mother Nature,

An inexhaustible process supporting this adventure.

A pattern in every form, standard of the norm,

It's a ceaseless study repeated throughout history.

Our standard application of discipline

Is applied as a device for sacrifice,

Especially when used to romanticize and seduce

And encourage others to justify its misuse in segments

Of society that idolize ideals of youth and beauty, usurping

Idealized ideals, concepts, and values that are trustworthy.

Or, when discipline becomes a war mechanism

Reducing populations in the name of patriotism.

Another face to discipline and competition:
When obsession defines a particular race, a
Connection linked by association of ideas and
Attachment to emotions forged in expressive ways.
It's also another way of ritualistic cleansing as
Exampled in the ocean and animal kingdom.
A characteristic of conformity displayed,
Personality trait found in DNA.

Discipline and competition inextricably twined
Fundamental elements in life's design. When
Emotion is consumed by desire to gain expression
Obsession creates situation under suitable conditions.
Leaders and followers from every corner on earth
Re-enact this play repeatedly from time of their birth.
Pattern of conformity perceived in every square,
An instrumental engine generating new ideas.

Discipline must be encouraged for competition to flourish,

Structures built on trust with elements that are robust.

Trust is essential to fuel persuasion, a

Foundation empowering all relations; it's a

System that binds beliefs from ancient times, a

Profound feeling of confidence and reliability; a

Complete and consummate spirit in nature's design,

Trust is the all encompassing will of the Divine.

Trust and Faith

Trust, as in faith, is difficult to fathom,
Hazardous situation if you're seated at the bottom.
If misplaced, its results may confound you
If unfounded, then you may be misguided.
Trust is transformed by many disguises,
Its lessons are habitually tested by the wisest.
If practiced sparingly, keen judgment may be earned,
If squandered irresponsibly, despair will be discerned.

Trust is an amazingly believable affair
One can be convinced consistently all year.
Discipline in presentation, competition, and reputation
Showcase qualities gained by successful salesmen.
Excellent craftsmanship displays superior abilities,
Concentration and determination dedicated to quality.
Belief in one's skills, technique and training
Reveals that trust and faith is confidence unfailing.

Faith is having strong sense of belief in the unknown.
Each breath taken, each word spoken, begs the question
Is life a dream, a vision, or talent that has grown?
Our senses provide tools we use so well,
Taste and touch, sight, sound and smell.
Such commonplace talent fills the world with hope –
Fabric created from ancient myths and jokes; a process
Our personality demands, a web woven by our own hands.

Faith is reflected in our confidence, our inner sense of security,
Firm knowledge that our purpose here is one of creativity.
Each of us creates the world we live in – our personal reality,
Expressed through our individuality – our own needs,
Desires, our emotional intent, fuelled by our own ambition:
An intense motivation unique in each expression to stamp
And imprint the indelible marks of our fingerprints;
To make our world harmonious, one without discontent.

Faith and Confidence

Faith and confidence – our twin offerings,
Sustain us through the raging battle and gruelling race.
The sun has its golden glow; faith is our strongest ace,
Confidence empowers us to set the winning pace.
Our eagerness to enter the fray, to play,
Tests our passion and commitment every day; but
Our aspirations and joyousness overcome our dismay
As we fight with our last breath to stay.

Faith is a foundational factor in our own biology,
Our cells replicate endlessly and joyously in the
Belief of growing and developing with high energy.
They reproduce with abandon,
Focused only on their own creations:
Creating all organs in our body, our skin
And all material needed to maintain them. That is
Faith in action with confidence in its own production.

Confidence and faith, partners in our pact for survival.
A strong belief in ourselves, our instincts and abilities
Cultivates confidence in creation of our own reality.
Our interests and activities, occupations we pursue,
Enlighten our perspective, broaden our world view. These
Acts of faith encourage us to accumulate knowledge,
Erect monumental structures in celebration of our courage.
Faith is our cornerstone, our anchor wherever we may roam.

Strength in our confidence is a measure of our faith,
Our aspiration and our courage to pursue bold ideas.
We develop ideas from our image of our self,
Often that image is a reflection from someone else.
Confidence is believing in our own potential to shine,
In our intuition, our insight, all aspects of our mind.
These are tools we use to create our own designs:
Our uniqueness, our individuality, our own stamp in time.

Emotion is inextricable from our faith and confidence
It projects the energy we birth – oh, such innocence!
We blast from the unknown into the present with a
Noisy determination to transform every continent.
Faith is the agent that changes every story
Propelling us from infancy, aging to maturity.
Confidence cushions us transporting to fame and glory
Allowing every experience its eternal history.

Confidence builds on a foundation of faith,
In its rambunctious nature and quest for new ideas.
Instincts provide us and impulses guide us to stretch,
To reach, and to be flexible in numerous ways. Each
Repeated action becomes a stronger plan, especially
When based on positive outcome of event beforehand.
Success is the goal, always the higher reach,
Confidence inspires us as a truth we constantly seek.

Responsibility

Relationship is loaded with many responsibilities,
Love and partnership, and other shared economies:
Knowledge, expectation, need, are mere normalities,
Tension, dependency, obligation, forced formalities.
Relationship is connection, contrast, sympathetic strand
A twine that binds every imaginable thing to man.
Our capacity is challenged by emotional moods, our
Flexibility, endurance, are responsible for paths pursued.

Responsibility is fundamental to independent thought,
Characteristic of moral principles philosophically taught.
It's a quality inherent in all relations, a foundation –
The essence of life in all of its formations.
Responsibility is responsible for every given in life: every
System, every process, every natural or imagined device
Is accountable to principles the laws of nature provide. An
Interrelatedness as natural as intuiting the stars as our guide.

Our well-being depends on how responsibly we survive,
Our energy, our thoughts, sustenance needed to stay alive.
Activities we pursue create associations anew, establishing,
Cementing connections, bonding process very much like glue.
As individuals, we are each responsible for our own actions,
Whether our logic justifies it, or
We're simply persuaded to follow some other rhetoric, our
Final decision should be guided by responsible consideration.

Our passage through life relates
To our willingness to survive. Passion
We bring, our committed offerings
Are all efforts to revive
Our dedication to our lives.
Time spent here should be
Savoured with positive care
As a joyful event, divinely sent.

Our Highest Values

Life in action should be lived
With abandoned passion;
Friendships selected with
Intelligent determination.
Occupations we pursue should
Be from a point of view where
Understanding and compassion
Are our highest values.

Approaching opportunities –
Challenges and solutions
From the perspective of
Going on an adventure, would
Heighten every moment bringing
Much joy and anticipated pleasure,
Making every endeavour a wonder,
And fun to discover.

Stories we tell are culled from a wishing well,
Each tale an adventure invented without censure.
It's the realization that challenges and solutions
Are designed to include tension, and test
Issues with our knowledge and comprehension
Of values and ideas, concepts and perspectives
Viewed in numerous ways, all accommodated by
A system responsible for the greatest displays.

Responsibility, delightful strand weaved into nature's plan,
Every element carrying its own ethical stance.
The wind blows as a gale force or light breeze
Ocean waves arch stormily or with frolicking ease.
Each occurs as a service doing its duty happily,
Responding to tides and currents accordingly.
In nature's design elements are most kind
Each form supporting humanity with integrity.

Responsibility, conscious quality within man,

An attribute applied or ignored on demand.

We are responsible for the planet we inhabit

The planet's response is sumptuous and automatic.

Integrity is bolstered by our own inner sanctuary; a

Bold and profound connection, an extreme emotion,

Principal strength in all matter universally; it's an

Eternal spring that radiates throughout all creation.

Integrity

Integrity is our moral honesty –
Our inner level of incorruptibility that
Bubbles through each individual's responsibility
To accept or reject ideas and actions, virtue and
Kindness that dwell within our own sanctuary.
Our moral stance is an integral part of our divinity –
An instinctive feature within all living things
And a conscious attribute within human beings.

Virtue is a distinction of our inner goodness, the
Highest measure of intensity of our own behaviour;
A constant reminder of our connection to the Divine
And an expression of our own faith and piousness.
Virtue and piety, components of our own integrity
Seeding our own pride and honesty. They are our
Fountains of satisfaction and stability,
Foundation sets for all of humanity.

Pride is a product of our own integrity,
Highest value placed on our own sensitivity;
A reflection of our own self-image and our solidarity
Uniting our compassion, our reasoning, our generousity.
Such qualities of excellence are built on self-respect,
A characteristic of nature that we faithfully project.
These bands of tension vibrate with sincere insistence
With an intensity that needs careful, constant adjustments.

Our sense of pride is fostered by our own accomplishments
Tasks performed to the fullest measure of our competence.
Such effort completes our own sense of fulfilment and
Raises our level of satisfaction to degrees of contentment.
This inner confidence motivates superior acts – repeated
Happenings reinforced by our fearlessness and self-respect.
Successful achievement keeps the circle intact
Mirroring the world as it twirls – a model project.

This naturally competitive streak
Energizes nature in its struggle to survive,
Challenging every position in every situation
To be relentless in its determination and its drive.
Such intensity of emotion is stirred by devotion and
Ambition to succeed in its desires and its needs. By
Standing staunchly with confidence, faith and integrity, each
Of us has the capacity to assume the mantle of responsibility.

Responsibility can be an onerous weight which
Many attempt but few successfully officiate.
Tensions and decisions that occur can carry
Consequences circumstances may not infer. How we
Weather these storms depend on our own temperament,
Our flexibility and our sincere intentions, which reveals
Our motives and our mental environment – elements of
Fear and resentment or satisfaction and contentment.

Nervous Energy

Our approach to responsibility may
Be viewed with an attitude of nervous energy.
This creates an imbalance in our confidence
And forms a perspective inclined to suspicion.
In such an instance our senses are hypnotized, our
Flexibility and ability to analyze is compromised.
At this point, we lose faith in our own capability:
In our own judgment and our own objectivity.

Such impairment then becomes our main concern,
Our focus now becomes a source of alarm.
Pressure and tension build steadily, illness
May develop if not treated compassionately.
These results reveal areas within our organizations
Where an individual's endurance and mental capacity
Are measured according to standardized categories,
And any imperfect fit is classified as an abnormality.

In all such instances across the various spectrums
Where human relations reveal scientific deviations
The question is, do we adjust our measuring systems
According to human need or scientific belief?
Evidence painstakingly reveals to what degree
Our fellowman is relating to his own individuality
In providing service and accommodating 'Special Needs',
Valuing human worth as the highest priority.

Our Value System

Our value system is our primary responsibility,
Our ultimate gift, one that is very praiseworthy
When all forms of life is given the highest category
And the greatest care becomes a normality.
Divisions and discriminations will be for other reasons not
Based on race or, for goodness sake! Who's going to heaven,
But on the calibre of the issues and solutions pursued, the
Depth of our emotion, compassion, understanding – virtues.

Our value system is our governing strength
Every individual has their own built in defence.
There may be some actions that we let slide
But there are other actions that attack our pride.
When such activities cause us inner concern,
It is to our value system that we turn.
Each of us knows to what extent
Our own moral flexibility is bent.

Every individual's value system is composed of many beliefs
Our needs, our desires and our ethical affinities.
Issues and concerns that each of us represent
Are complementary components of every event.
This larger perspective provides an organizational plan
And groups activities within a certain vibrational band.
This allows every action, every system, every process,
To share the scope of life across earth's span.

Various perspectives we bring to a situation
Relate entirely to the importance of our value system.
Every individual will have a different point of view
To facts and circumstances within their purview. If one's
Primary concern is centered on family responsibility
Then their opinions will be governed by parental duty.
If another's concern is focused on freedom and equality
Then a more expansive view will advocate for inclusivity.

These differing visions if collated together and
Viewed with a lens that shows patterning behaviour
Would reveal mathematically a balanced equation
Displaying sparkling facets found in every population.
These personalities are organized with energy, and with
Their potential possibilities exist within generalities.
Individuals with 'Special Needs' requirements command
Compassionate attention from our value system.

Our Journey

Our journey here is one filled with limitations
Characteristics that grant us differentiation.
These features force us to focus our attention
On captivating spirits willing to express them.
Such individuals evoke an emotional intensity,
Profound appreciation the world would never see;
This all-encompassing trait transforms humanity
Advertising its greatest qualities as spirituality.

Brave personalities are effusive in their affection
Electrifying the world by capturing its imagination;
Their need for normality circumvents convention
Requiring special treatment: a need for reinvention.
Such concentration – insightful and penetrating
Unifies the world anew, reinforcing and invigorating.
This spectacular style promotes a new understanding,
A driving force in habits, relations and communications.

This blending of positive values with our own intelligence
Stirs up a passionate reaction inspiring due diligence;
Conscientiousness geared to mixing empathy with science
Transforming formulas in the interest of new experience.
Astounding record-breaking performances set new limits,
Exhibiting competence and authority forming new habits;
This new confidence confirms our capacity for originality
Establishing new patterns of expression and creativity.

These new concepts pioneer progressive technology
Introducing outstanding products and terminology.
Brilliant ideas affectionately facilitate various lifestyles
Extending our liberty with autonomy unknown otherwise.
Our limitations then, are impacted to an enormous degree,
In many instances innovation has increased our longevity;
Such advancement demonstrates our courage and ingenuity,
Our excellence and flexibility in thinking revolutionary.

Our thoughts and ideas influence our relationships
Magnanimous opinions reflect positive sponsorship;
Our capacity to show compassion to our fellow man
Reveals depths of emotion our care commands.
Our industries depict the extent our needs are met
Our commitment to the cause shows in new projects,
Building alliances, supporting different commonalities
Strengthening the bonds of diversity cooperatively.

This exciting process is truly an all-encompassing affair
Embracing variety in innumerable and immeasurable ways;
Every individual has their own fascinating part to play
Communicating their own ambition each and every day.
These situations captivate us with occupational ideas
Converting emotional energy into dynamic displays;
Limitation provides opportunity for constant invention
Renewal of our purpose and continued socialization.

Golden Moments

Artists throughout the ages explore every relationship
Portraying emotions and feelings in their workmanship;
Such expressions of concentration show our sensitivity,
Aspects of personality in relation to our own individuality.
Our behaviour reveals the profundity of our moral terrain
Sympathy and concern or our grappling for personal gain;
These decisions distinguish us in our goals and aspirations,
Our wisdom and willingness to surrender despite the occasion.

As we pursue our path on our journey through this life
These aspects and possibilities act as a screening device
To encourage us in all our actions our potential to realize
Allowing every desire its opportunity to fulfill and to satisfy.
Our likes and dislikes present us with many golden moments
Cleverly guiding our course by agreement and entertainment,
Our fearlessness to face our foe summons all of our courage
Elevating us to higher rank, fortifying faith and confidence.

Sense of Daring

Any bold development increases our sense of daring
Boosting our self-esteem encouraging greater risk-taking.
This added responsibility stretches our own capacity: our
Conscientiousness, trustworthiness and personal reliability.
Our sense of self is challenged to the highest degree,
Our competence, our motivation and our own proficiency.
Such accountability can test the resolve and noble dignity
Of any individual who undertakes a level of higher authority.

We are assessed by importance we place on our performance,
Our genuineness, sacrifice, our meticulousness and vigilance;
Standards we set, rules that encourage respect and influence;
Our values – attitude and philosophy – make all the difference.
Our response to daily affairs shows-off our natural abilities,
Qualities that sustain us throughout our growth and maturity.
These traits remind us of our connection to every personality
Eccentricity shared by all of humanity to sculpt individuality.

Each of us has our own impressions about life to pursue,
Plans to develop, beliefs to test, and concepts to execute.
We show our personal courage in every independent action
Creating reality with confidence of our own conviction.
The universe supports every action, every thought in view
Encouraging every generation to succeed a tiny step or two.
Lessons we all are taught, are the foundation for the future
Pillars, our towers of strength, prime us for great adventure.

Sparkling Gems

Our fascination with life concentrates our passion for living,
Prodding us to pursue conduct contrary to traditional thinking.
The extent to which we trust this advice and plunge into being
Expresses our adventurousness and our penchant for inventing.
This dicey decision will only guarantee some brilliant insights
And marvellous adventures resulting in spectacular highlights,
Our need, desire, determination to follow through to the end
Will garner us much praise and adulation; enemies and friends.

Situations we encounter in striving to become our best
Challenge us to the maximum, a mental and physical test;
Self-image we nurture, our conscience, our code of morality
Is tempted in every endeavour to compromise its integrity;
If we keep focused unswervingly on accomplishing our plan
Obstacles will present no dilemma, Faith will take command.
Sparkling gems will reward us with facets of stunning clarity,
Skill and ability will be extended to include superior activity.

Surprise will be a constant factor on our mission in the maze,
Coincidence or self-confidence, our own new catchphrase.
These empowering developments rearrange our own ideas
Perceiving new thoughts, new visions, new goals and ambition.
Such shrewd ingenuity stretches our intellect and imagination
Affording us the luxury of thinking with extra-natural ability,
This genius-like quality supersedes other normal capability
Changing relationships with contemporaries, friends and family.

Navigating this new environment requires observing new signs,
Maintaining our equilibrium, celebrating gifts from the Divine;
With great enthusiasm we anticipate authentic sponsorship, a
Cheering section made up of happy and excited candidates;
In some instances our reception is met with uninspired applause
Dispirited faces full of disregard showing no joy in our reward.
At such times we remain composed, no frost will wither our rose,
Vibrant times for vibrant folks, vivacious hearts, vivacious hopes.

Concentration then is captivated by a more precise authority
Time is regulated by performance geared to a new expectancy,
Attention is given to pursuits that profit positive productivity
Admiration and affection won by all who champion proficiency.
Such virtuosity captures imagination of an approving audience
Impacting our cause as important while raising our prominence;
Badge of distinction propels us into a larger sphere of influence
Transforming our environment with the events of confluence.

Excitement

Demonstrating passion for a cause generates excitement
Everyone yields to the rhythm ignited by their commitment,
We all have our own feelings to organize and communicate
Spurred on by surroundings our situation illuminates.
All causes are purposefully designed to promote harmony –
Sympathy, sensitivity, feelings of shared accountability.
Such responsibility deepens awareness of our environment:
Urgent needs, complicated conditions, global disturbance.

Our response to any of these issues cannot be in isolation
Connecting to a cause involves engagement and reflection,
Our sympathy may be influenced by a special attraction
Commanding attention for the benefit of close relations.
Such opportunities allow us advantage to have fellowship
Appreciating reasons and occasions to participate,
These occurrences summon deep pockets of emotion
Awakening energy, adding intensity, force to the promotion.

Such enthusiasm is contagious throughout the population
Encouraging support to causes, fostering good relations,
Individuals from all walks of life and from every generation
Sacrifice activities to participate, working in cooperation.
Such dynamic spontaneity mushrooms everywhere – universal,
Uniting people and nations in efforts that should not be unusual;
Such drive and determination energize energetic decisions,
Undertaking larger projects aiming for massive contribution.

Under these circumstances, a collective consciousness
Comes together to promote good health and healing awareness.
These activities ricochet as great movements around the world
Bringing us closer to each other, achieving shared goals.
Such harmonizing of feelings support a softening mentality
Promoting positive approach respecting problem-solving ability.
On this level, unanimously, our hearts communicate as one
Spreading warmth and goodwill, benevolence under the sun.

Such genuine and influential feelings of affection
Bathe the universe in a glow with generous disposition,
Casting spells on every nation supporting harmonious relations
And cultivating within cultures a blending of separate divisions.
This meeting of the mind creates energy of an unbeatable kind
Inspiring efforts around the globe searching for reliable cures
To confer with each other and speak with singular voice their
Approach to many challenges, their decisions and their choice.

Such growth and understanding underscore a need for unity and
Within competitive fields nurture thoughts of friendly solidarity;
This type of cohesion is necessary across the board, a
Mobilization of forces to advance us to our desired reward.
Such communication increases our mental activity, organizing,
Synchronizing, meeting agreed standards with consistency.
This type of orchestration confirms a sublime intelligence –
Extraordinary conscientiousness with superb awareness.

Personalities with such meticulousness surpass limitations
Breaking barriers, setting new standards for contemplation.
This approach constantly reveals new areas of discovery
New thoughts, new ideas, new characteristics and abilities.
With this expansion our lives become lively with spontaneity
Our needs and desires mushroom and assume a new urgency –
Opportunities for expression, pleasurable experiences,
Ground-breaking decisions, pioneering ambition as occurrences.

A wealth of ideas surrounds us ceaselessly and continuously
Prodding us into taking action thoughtfully or instinctively,
Such unpredictability challenges our notions of normalcy, every
Where and at every level offers a sense of unconventionality.
This state of being advances us all individually and universally,
Heightening our desire to compete in adventurous activity
Developing our courage, skills, talent, our sense of bravery,
Increasing our knowledge of ourselves and our own ingenuity.

Such emotion and perception is not unusual for mankind
Everyone experiences their own unique and distinct design,
Our personal expression is exclusive to our own character
Our own idiosyncratic approach to everything that matters;
We all excel in our own exciting way, quietly or exuberantly,
Each of us fashions our own patterns, our own image on display,
This use of our energy extends our capacity and abilities
Modelling for others' goals and success needed in every society.

Special Needs

Personality, as a principle, is difficult to fathom,
Everyone is governed by intensity of their emotions.
These flickering feelings are energy in motion
Demanding attention by the forms of their expression.
Shades of anger, love, or humour, dominates
The landscape that portrays their behaviour.
Elements of fear, understanding, compassion
Discover in us the depths of our own emotions.

From these tensions we unravel many threads
Staining them with ink colour of our own temperament.
These threads mix and merge in exuberant displays
Creating colourful situations in dynamic ways.
Every situation attracts its own degree of energy
Subjected to analytical scrutiny of mental activity,
These tensions contain their own thirst for equality –
Pressure exerted upon all of humanity.

Bombardment of patterns and intricate designs
Can sometimes overwhelm and boggle the mind,
These pockets of energy can create questions of doubt
Rifts in confidence, competence and instincts with clout.
Circumstances requiring our immediate attention
May tax and overburden our fluid emotions,
Under such conditions we require a time-out,
To center ourselves, breathing deeply, in and out.

Personality, in its composition, is difficult to measure,
Competing elements seeking value as preferred treasure.
Emotions motivated into action by our inner desires are
Organized with urgency and intelligence we all admire.
Within these features tension is the triggering device
Creating strain in unequal portions with dramatic advice,
Emphasizing issues to which our compassion should be drawn –
'Special Needs' within the population to be considered as norm.

Energy in Action

It is within the nature of our nature
Under the stimulus of pain
To be motivated towards a greater gain;
Competitive elements, always in a conquering vein
Seek to triumph over discomfort with intent to reign.
This striving spirit exults and exalts
With ferocious energy its tasks to perform –
Energy in action – purpose for which we all were born.

Translating energy, our efforts cannot be denied;
Changing matter into objects suitable for us to survive;
Engaging with the elements our planet lovingly provides
Fascinates us every moment, our attachment is multiplied.
This profound dedication has a mesmerizing effect –
Hypnotizing us, capturing our energy,
Blinding us to the point where we cannot imagine
Other realms or alien organizations.

Optimism

Spheres of music and mathematics supply
Organizing principles sounds and formulas abide.
These shape our world, our environment, our idyll,
Influencing our passions, articulating our lives.
In this atmosphere variety is prioritized
Balancing our equilibrium, bolstering our quality of life;
Such sources of energy are resources for our planet
Fuelling our thoughts, our ideas, and our habits.

In our system we explore many concepts pursuing
Particular ideas for social or political benefit;
In this setting, segments of the population,
For personal reasons, follow their aspiration and
Establish business relations boasting political affiliation.
These events fulfill a humanitarian need expressing
A sense of caring by sowing philanthropic seeds –
Compassion and sympathy, a benefit to charity.

These traits influence our temperament, a natural function;
Combination of instincts and emotions that foster passion.
These passions organize our daily habits
Revealing their strengths as behavioural characteristics.
These characteristics are frequently on display in
Events and situations in which we all participate, such
Situations engage us with varying degrees of complexity,
Either fleetingly or prolonged, or as revisited memory.

As our emotions mix and merge in swirling patterns
Aspects of our personality whirl into energetic action,
Polished elements are pulled vividly into prominence
Affecting relations existing under the circumstance.
Peaceful situations agitated by an urgent desire
Can sometimes change by the excitement of fire;
Such confrontational aspects ignite the mind
Refreshing the atmosphere, recasting the design.

Individuality

Every toss of the emotions spins a new perspective
Allowing every personality opportunity to be objective;
Deep-rooted feelings are called into play,
Emotional strands in flux, dazzling in display.
Every individual asserts their own distinctive character
Aligning their emotional strands with issues that matter.
Subtle pressures, balancing techniques, create the unique in
Every individual granting each personality opportunity to speak.

Personality, as a principle, is difficult to fathom
Elements of its composition swiftly shifting in action
Converting their expression with knowledge and wisdom.
These daily battles are scenes filled with sage advice
Encouraging us to absorb information to be wise.
Organizing these strands into a competitive whole
Individuals are believed to be fulfilling their role.
Personalities, converters of energy, are magnificent to behold.

Review Requested:

If you loved this book, would you please provide
a review at Amazon.com?

CPSIA information can be obtained at www.ICGtesting.com
Printed in the USA
LVOW06*2053190215

427619LV00001B/6/P

9 781631 353925